# Charles Darwin

## Alan Gibbons
### Illustrated by Leo Brown

KINGFISHER

# ᴷ KINGFISHER

First published 2008 by Kingfisher
This edition published 2011 by Kingfisher
an imprint of Macmillan Children's Books
a division of Macmillan Publishers Limited
20 New Wharf Road, London N1 9RR
Basingstoke and Oxford
Associated companies throughout the world
www.panmacmillan.com

ISBN 978-0-7534-3223-5

Consultant: Professor James Secord, Cambridge University, Director
of the Darwin Correspondence Project (www.darwinproject.ac.uk)

Copyright © Macmillan Publishers Ltd 2008
Text copyright © Alan Gibbons 2008
Illustration copyright © Leo Brown 2008

JB
DAR

9 8 7 6 5 4 3 2 1

1TR/0511/LFG/UG/140MA/C

A CIP catalogue record for this book is available from the British Library.

Printed in China

*This is one of the surveying instruments that Darwin took on the Beagle voyage. The photographs in the diary chapter of this book show plants, creatures and objects that Darwin saw on his travels.*

*Darwin preserved the animals he caught in alcohol or chemicals in glass jars. These reptiles are part of his collection.*

# Contents

# JAMES'S DIARY

James Kincaid's diary extracts
tell of his time as a ship's boy
aboard the HMS *Beagle* from 1832
to 1836. The *Beagle*'s voyage around South
America and nearby islands was to be an amazing
journey of discovery. Charles Darwin joined the
expedition because he wanted to be the ship's naturalist,
studying the animals and plants of this unknown place. When
he returned home to England, he developed his observations
into important new scientific theories about the natural world.

AUTHOR'S NOTE: James and his pet are fictional characters that
I've created. They were not on the *Beagle*'s voyage, but the
people in James's diary did exist, and the events described
are based on what actually happened.

# January, 1832

Today I received a gift. You may not think that's such a great surprise, but the man who gave it to me is a wealthy gentleman and I am but a volunteer boy sailor, ten years old. My benefactor's name is Mr Charles Darwin of Shrewsbury, England. Let me tell you how he came to present me with his gift, the journal in which I am writing this diary.

Our ship, the HMS *Beagle*, is some weeks out of Plymouth, on a journey to map and chart the coasts of South America and Tierra del Fuego, its southernmost point. The master of the vessel is Captain Robert Fitzroy. Mr Darwin is travelling with us as his guest. This is the first time we have touched land since we set sail. The crew are clearly glad to disembark and look around. Some are gathering fresh fruit to keep scurvy at bay.

MIDSHIPMAN KING

HMS *BEAGLE*

CHARLES DARWIN

CAPTAIN ROBERT FITZROY

JAMES KINCAID

Our present port of call is the island of St Jago. It is situated 450 miles from the coast of Africa. I have never seen the like of this place. The land is very dry – we've been told that it hasn't rained for an entire year! Mr Darwin looks most relieved to be walking on solid ground once more. By all accounts, he has had a terrible passage. Captain Fitzroy told his officers that the crossing of the Bay of Biscay was the worst he has experienced.

*Mr Darwin made notes about each bird he saw on St Jago.*

Poor Mr Darwin has spent most days rocking in his hammock, suffering dreadfully from seasickness. Midshipman King, who shares a cabin with him, says he even clears the cabin table sometimes so that he can lie flat. He has little experience of life at sea and is yet to find his sea legs.

But there is more to it than mere relief at setting foot on firm ground. Mr Darwin seems thrilled by the lush, green valleys, the coconut palms and orange trees that we see everywhere. How different this world is to the one we left at home. I saw Mr Darwin in the market this morning. He had just bought a banana and was sampling it. He didn't seem to know what to make of the taste at first. Finally, he decided it was too sweet. Later in the day a flock of strange birds took flight, fifty or sixty of them in all. Mr Darwin told me they were guinea fowl. That was the first time he ever spoke to me. It wouldn't be the last during our stay on the island. Though I am no gentleman, he seems happy to involve me in his explorations.

*Notebooks are essential for cataloguing the discoveries on the journey.*

We moved on to Quail Island. Mr Darwin is collecting every creature he can find. He says that walking around these tropical islands has been like giving a blind man eyes. He is starting to see the world in a different way. This afternoon he scoured the rock pools along the coast. He was tremendously excited by an octopus he found. He watched with great wonder when it changed colour as it tried to escape. He was soon scribbling down notes and sketches in a small book. He has a tremendous enthusiasm for nature's treasures.

*To keep the octopus from rotting, Mr Darwin preserved it in alcohol.*

When he noticed me watching, he produced a second book from his pocket and offered it to me. He asked me if I knew how to read and write. When I told him very firmly that I did, he was pleased. He suggested that I keep my own diary of the voyage. Well, I protested strongly saying he shouldn't be giving his precious notebooks away to all and sundry, but he finally persuaded me to take it. Secretly, I am absolutely delighted to have it.

Back on board ship that night, he showed everybody how the octopus he had captured could glow in the dark. He was like a child himself, thrilled by his find. He was most disappointed to hear that it wasn't a new discovery. Nonetheless, he is putting together his scientific discoveries, making notes, and cataloguing finds. For a man considering entering the Church when he returns to England, he seems set on a very different career. Surely he was born to be a man of science and exploration?

For the first time since I signed up
for the voyage, I am beginning to feel
at home. I have fallen in love with the
ship. The *Beagle* is going to be my
home for the next few years. She is a
ninety-footer with a capacity of 242 tons.
She has three masts and some cannon.
According to Captain Fitzroy, that makes
her a ten-gun brig. Some of the men say
she is really little more than a wreck,
a broken-down coastal carrier.

I don't care what they say. I love it
when I am sent up to loose the sails.
It is so exhilarating to be high above the
deck with the wind in my face and the
sea spray stinging my eyes! You can see
far, far across the glittering ocean.

I expect the *Beagle* to introduce me to the most marvellous sights and adventures. Joining her crew wasn't such a difficult decision. I was orphaned some years since and have been living with my uncle in Wapping, selling supplies to the seafaring folk. My uncle and his wife have always considered me something of a burden, so I was glad to trade them for my new family, the crew of the *Beagle*.

In addition to the crew, there are others on board. There is Mr Darwin, of course. Captain Fitzroy chose him because he is a gentleman of good breeding and a suitable companion for the captain. Then there are an instrument maker, a missionary and an artist. Because of these guests, the deck is covered in their boxes and instruments. The missionary, Mr Richard Matthews, is charged with returning three natives, Fuegians from Tierra del Fuego, to their home at the tip of South America.

Captain Fitzroy brought the natives to England on a previous journey and they have been living there for some time. They even had an audience with His Majesty the King and Queen Adelaide. I have seen the natives fleetingly from time to time, but I will write about them in greater detail when I know more about them.

As I lie here in my hammock, watching the oil lamp swinging to and fro, casting its yellow glow, I can hear the prow cutting through the waves, the snap of the wind in the sails and the creak of the rigging. No doubt Mr Darwin is suffering from seasickness again, but once he is recovered he will unearth more of nature's secrets. My hope is that he will let me accompany him.

It is our third day on the islands. Mr Darwin has become fascinated by a horizontal white rock some forty-five feet above the water. He believes that this layer is an old sand beach, raised up in the recent past by the force of a volcano. It can't have been very long ago, because the shells are just the same as those we collected by the ocean today. Mr Darwin seems to be able to see all the changes the land has gone through in his mind's eye. Later, he even showed me how the volcano had erupted, baking the seashells into the hard, white layer. How he can work this out merely by looking at the hillside and examining the rocks and soil I can't imagine, but with every day that passes he seems to become more sure of himself. He thinks he can tell the story of the islands from these signs. Mr Darwin is either very clever or very fanciful.

He was sitting on the beach eating tamarinds and biscuit for lunch, and gazing at the tidal pools at his feet, when he smiled suddenly. One of the men asked him what he was thinking. He said quietly that one day he was going to write a book about the natural history of the island.

# February–July, 1832

*Mr Darwin collected a huge range of creatures in his nets, including many crabs.*

The days continue to be warmer and the waves less choppy than when we crossed the Bay of Biscay. The sails ripple lazily in the gentle breeze. Mr Darwin spends much of the day trawling the waters for plankton and jellyfish. He uses the most peculiar contraptions to catch his creatures and study them. I have rarely seen any man more excited about so simple an occupation as fishing. When he is dipping for his samples, his eyes sparkle. He sometimes asks how my diary is progressing. I tell him that I am keeping it up to date when I can, filling it with my thoughts and sketches. He seems pleased. Of course, I try not to take up too much of his time. He is, after all, the captain's guest and a fine country gentleman. I have heard it said that he is related to Mr Josiah Wedgwood, the famous potter. I have a feeling Captain Fitzroy would be most displeased if he thought I was pestering Mr Darwin. I must be respectful or the captain will lose patience with me.

I have good reason to be wary of the captain. I remember well my first experience of discipline at sea. I was roused early in the voyage by the shrieks of sailors being flogged. The captain ordered that four men be lashed with the cat-o'-nine-tails. It cut their backs to shreds. It turned out that they were being punished for drunkenness, insolence and neglect of duty. Five others were clapped in leg irons. The captain was sending out a message. He is prepared to handle the crew with a firm hand. Since that day I have been careful to do my duty well. I don't want to suffer a beating like those men. I still remember the look on Mr Darwin's face as he watched the floggings. He was as disturbed as I. It seems we think alike about many things.

I have had a chance to observe the three Fuegians. All three of them are quite short in stature and copper-skinned. The oldest goes by the name of York Minster. Fancy being named after a church! His real name is El'leparu. He is a quiet, brooding kind of man. He is very protective of the only female in the group, Fuegia Basket. Her real name is Yockushlu. She is very quiet in her ways but quick to learn languages. She has picked up English and some Spanish and Portuguese. The crew's favourite is Jemmy Button, also known as Orundellico. He is a gentle, fun-loving man who enjoys telling jokes. He is very proud of his English appearance and he always dresses in smart London clothes. He wears his hair neatly cut and oiled.

It seems the captain took them to England as a kind of experiment. He wanted to see how they would adapt to English ways and how they would behave when returned to their own land. I have often heard Captain Fitzroy and Mr Darwin discussing the Fuegians, debating how strong the influence of British society will prove to be. I can't help but wonder how they will fare. How easy will it be for them to fit into their former world after so long away? What if they have got too used to our English ways? Still, our arrival in Tierra del Fuego is some months in the future. We will see what happens when we get there.

LEG IRONS

JEMMY BUTTON

YORK MINSTER

FUEGIA BASKET

16

Very occasionally, the captain relaxes discipline a little. Today was an example. Mr Darwin had to undergo quite an ordeal. It is called Crossing the Line. One of the crew painted himself green and played the part of the sea god Neptune, King of the Deep. The youngest volunteers on board, Musters and I, were got up in our own war paint. We pranced around while the other men egged us on. For just a few moments it didn't matter who were the officers and who the men in their charge. The world had been turned upside down. We actually shaved some of the officers. We even poured buckets of salt water over the heads of Mr Darwin and Captain Fitzroy, something that would have been unthinkable on any other day. It was great fun, but after an hour or so, of course, everything had gone back to normal, with the officers giving us orders and we obeying them without question.

The moment we arrived in Bahia, Brazil, Mr Darwin was off on his travels. He sees the voyage of the *Beagle* less as a sea journey and more as a series of adventures on land joined by quick hops across the ocean. He came back, as he always does, with many specimens in his jars and boxes. There are beetles and spiders and the most brightly coloured butterflies you ever saw in your life. He seemed thrilled at being caught in a tropical rainstorm that soaked him through in seconds. He found the whole experience very exciting. He wants the lands we explore to be as different from the countryside near his native Shrewsbury as can be.

His high spirits didn't last long. He was soon horrified by the spectacle of slavery in the territories of Brazil. The slaves are flogged much more savagely than the sailors on the *Beagle* have ever been.

I already knew that Mr Darwin was appalled by any kind of cruelty. I've seen his face when the captain punishes members of the crew. It seems that Darwin's family are great opponents of the slave trade. Mr Darwin believes that the poor wretches we saw shackled are men and women like the rest of us and have the same feelings as anyone else. Captain Fitzroy is of a different opinion. He believes they are reasonably well treated and as happy as if they were free people. He can't see any difference between the slaves and the factory hands who work for Mr Darwin's relative, Mr Wedgwood, in his famous pottery factory.

This difference of opinion led to a furious argument one evening. We sailors could hear it up on deck. To our amazement, a whisper went round the ship the next morning that Captain Fitzroy had apologized for losing his temper. None of us had ever dreamed that a man as proud as the captain would apologize to anyone. It seems that the two gentlemen have agreed not to discuss slavery again so that they can avoid quarrelling over the issue.

Mr Darwin has seen a fish called a blenny. This is a drawing of it.

He is a very clever gentleman, though not so clever he can't be caught out by the sailors' mischievous humour. On April Fool's Day one of them called out: "Darwin, did you ever see a Grampus?" Well, Mr Darwin came rushing on deck in great excitement, imagining he was about to see some unknown species of animal, only to discover an empty sea. The crew had tremendous fun at his expense.

On the way from Bahia to Rio de Janeiro we passed through a stretch of sea which was stained bright red. We all wondered about this strange sight until Mr Darwin explained that the colour came about because of millions of tiny creatures swimming about. No matter how hard I stared I could see nothing but a crimson stain on the surface of the ocean.

When we docked at Rio, Captain Fitzroy ordered that the *Beagle* be caulked and painted in preparation for our onward journey. This would mean quite a long spell onshore while repairs were carried out. During that time Mr Darwin rented a house nearby. From Rio he has sent many boxes of specimens home to England. He certainly meant what he said about telling nature's story. It is a great task but I think Mr Darwin will be equal to it. He doesn't save everything for his collections, of course. One day he and Captain Fitzroy amused themselves scrambling over the rocks on the seashore, killing seabirds for the pot. They killed many noddies and boobies. Mr Darwin said the birds were so stupid they could have killed many more. I felt quite sorry for the poor creatures.

While we toiled preparing the *Beagle* for
the next stage of our journey, Mr Darwin
went exploring the forests, looking for
birds, monkeys and sloths; parrots,
toucans and alligators. He describes the
forest as a temple stocked by the god of
nature. It is a remarkable place with its
eternal insect chorus and grainy sunlight.
Creepers twist hither and thither while
parasitic orchids sprout everywhere,
sucking water from the other plants.
Mr Darwin continues to be upset by
the keeping of slaves, though he doesn't
mention it to the captain. One lady he
met admitted that she uses a thumbscrew
to crush the fingers of her female slaves
if they upset her. Such cruelty
appals our naturalist.

# July-August, 1832

*The bolas are two balls, one on either end of a rope. They are swung around, and then thrown to wrap around a creature's legs and capture it.*

We are at sea once more. Mr Darwin's nets and trawls are everywhere, hanging over the side of the ship. He spends hours poring over his books, staring through his microscope, and making reams of notes, but something happened this afternoon that brought him up on deck in a hurry. We came across a shoal of porpoises. There were hundreds of them leaping over the waves, often jumping clean out of the water. There were times when you would think they could fly. They entertained us for many minutes, criss-crossing the sea in front of the bow. We were disappointed when they finally let us be.

There was some excitement when we arrived in the harbour of Buenos Aires. A guard ship fired on us.

This was a sign of things to come. When we reached Bahia Blanca, we discovered that there was a lot of fighting between the Indians and an Argentine general, a ruthless man called de Rosas. It seems his army is set on exterminating the Indians. It is said they are even prepared to massacre women in cold blood!

War or no war, Mr Darwin iscontinuing his studies of the land, the plants and the animals of South America. He has been very fascinated by the local ostrich, the rhea. The horsemen, or gauchos, catch these flightless birds by flinging two balls held by threads. Mr Darwin had a go at the bolas, as they are called. He swung them round his head just as he had seen the gauchos do. Unfortunately, he hadn't got the hang of the contraption and managed to catch his own horse in the process! The gauchos roared with laughter. They said they had seen men catch all kinds of animals, but nobody had ever caught himself before. The incident was embarrassing, but it didn't put Mr Darwin off hunting. The ship's crew have dined on fresh tuna, turtle, shark and barracuda. We have also eaten deer, ostrich and armadillo. Sometimes I think Mr Darwin prefers eating nature to telling its story!

# August - November 1832

*Mr Darwin found many fossil bones. These are the foot bones of a Macrauchenia, which was a kind of large llama that lived millions of years ago.*

We have made a great discovery. Rounding a headland called Punta Alta yesterday, Captain Fitzroy and Mr Darwin came across some broken bones and shells embedded in the gravel beds. The two men were soon digging furiously with their bare hands. The bones turned out to be fossils. The captain and his guest ordered several of us to return with them today to chip the fossil bones loose. Soon we uncovered the teeth and bones of several very strange animals, which Darwin thinks were probably a kind of rhinoceros from a bygone era. Looking at these fossils, it was obvious to everyone that these animals had to be extinct. We had seen nothing like them roaming the Argentine plains. The story of nature must be longer and more mysterious than I had imagined. Mr Darwin seems to be puzzling over it. How can animals from past and present be so similar in some ways and so very different in others?

# December 1832-January 1833

As we approached Tierra del Fuego, we witnessed some huge humpback whales churning the ocean. One whale leapt almost entirely clear of the waves. Later, an albatross wheeled above us. It was very graceful, content to ride the breeze, like some king of the skies.

As we approached the Fuegians' homeland, fires started to spring up. Soon we caught sight of the inhabitants running along the shore in great excitement. Their bodies were painted red and white, and they were wearing hardly a scrap of clothing. We looked first at the three Fuegians on board, Jemmy Button, York Minster and Fuegia Basket, then at these people following us. Mr Darwin was fascinated that the three Fuegians could transform themselves into English citizens in such a short time. He is convinced that they will probably transform back again just as easily once they are returned to the forest, an idea that upsets Captain Fitzroy. According to him, civilization is a very fragile thing indeed.

Jemmy has been reunited with his brother and mother, back in the land from which he came. That doesn't stop us being very sad to leave the Fuegians in their homeland. They have been our companions ever since England. We will miss them greatly.

# September 1833

I have just returned from an excursion inland. Captain Fitzroy allowed me to accompany Mr Darwin on a long expedition across the pampas. It is wonderful to ride over the vast plains and sleep under the stars. We met General de Rosas and his gauchos along the way. The gauchos wear their hair long over the shoulders of their brightly coloured costumes. When they walk about, their spurs jangle loudly. They never remove the daggers that poke out menacingly from their belts. They escorted us across one particularly dangerous part of the pampas where we saw deer and ostriches. We roasted an ostrich one night and ate it around the camp fire. We also discovered more fossil bones. Mr Darwin said they belonged to a Mastodon (an elephant-like creature), but sadly they were too soft and powdery to be removed from the earth. He spent several days wondering how some species died out while others seemed to thrive a good while longer.

Now that our time travelling across the immense, open plains is at an end, we are turning our minds once more to Tierra del Fuego. Captain Fitzroy intends to continue charting the coast while he makes his way back to the spot where we left the Fuegians. He wishes to know how they have fared in the meantime, especially Jemmy Button, who was always the crew's favourite.

*The gauchos' spurs are attached to their boot heels and are used to guide a horse when riding.*

# March 1834

Jemmy is now married. His wife came with him to meet us, accompanied by Jemmy's brother, known to everyone on board the *Beagle* as Tommy Button. Before we left Woollya Cove for the last time, there was an exchange of gifts. The captain gave Jemmy a set of clothes while Jemmy gave him some otter skins. For Mr Darwin there were two spearheads. The whole crew lined up to shake Jemmy's hand as he said his farewells. As I watched his short figure vanish in the distance, I had a lump in my throat. We would all like to believe that one day some British seaman might crawl up on the shore after a shipwreck and find himself looking up into the smiling face of Jemmy Button.

O n our return to Woollya Cove, where we last left the Fuegians, we saw three canoes approaching the *Beagle*. We did not recognize any of the occupants at first. Then one of them raised his hand to his head in a kind of salute and we realized it was Jemmy Button. Captain Fitzroy and Mr Darwin were dismayed to see that he had become very thin and was wearing native clothing, in other words very little at all! Captain Fitzroy ordered that Jemmy be given some clothes so that he could eat at the captain's table like an English gentleman. Jemmy was soon using a knife and fork, and acting as if he had never been away.

TOMMY BUTTON

JEMMY BUTTON

JEMMY'S WIFE

# July 1834 - June 1835

We have reached Chile. After our visit to Tierra del Fuego and the bleak Falkland Islands, the sight of the glittering Pacific Ocean, the bright sun, blue sky and cloud-wreathed Andes lifts the spirits. As Mr Darwin put it, nature is sparkling with life. The volcano of Aconcagua is huge, towering to a height of 23,000 feet. It is the highest peak in the Americas. It fairly took my breath away. When you walk through the countryside, the flowers and shrubs give off wonderful perfumes. If you brush against a plant, your clothes will be scented with its aroma.

While we were surveying the nearby island of Chiloe, we witnessed a remarkable sight as three volcanoes erupted. At first all we could see was Mount Osorno spouting clouds of thick smoke. But there were more dramatic sights to come. The eruption lasted into the early hours of the following morning and nobody on board thought about going to bed that night.

If we thought the havoc wrought by wild nature was at an end, we were wrong. A great earthquake has followed the eruption of the volcanoes. The earth started rocking and shuddering. The vibrations only lasted a matter of minutes, but the effects on the local towns and villages was devastating. When we called at the town of Concepción, most of the buildings were razed to the ground. Beautiful churches have crumbled away completely. The town was nothing but a mass of rubble and timbers. Enormous cracks and fissures mark the earth all around.

*The smaller tortoises are about the size of a dinner plate, but others are the size of a table!*

Some while later we came across the island's biggest inhabitants, the huge Galápagos tortoises. We had been trudging through the weedy vegetation when we came across a kind of path between the cinders and the cacti. Turning up one of these paths, we finally met a pair of tortoises face to face. They must have weighed at least two hundred pounds each. To hungry sailors that means two hundred pounds of meat, of course. Many of these tortoises do end up in the pot, but not the pair we encountered that particular day. We were more interested in them as living creatures. As we approached, one was eating a cactus. The other gave a grumpy hiss and walked away. I tried riding its back but, though the tortoise didn't seem at all concerned or even aware that I was perched on its shell, I was unable to balance and kept slipping off and landing with a thump on my bottom. Midshipman King also had a go at riding the tortoise, but he ended up sprawled in an embarrassed heap just as I had.

On Albermarle Island we came across a second species of iguana. In contrast to its cousin on Chatham Island, this is a land-based reptile. It is just as unaccustomed to men as the seagoing iguanas on Chatham Island. Mr Darwin watched one of them burying itself in a burrow. When it was half-way underground, he pulled its tail. The iguana emerged to see what was the matter. It clearly wanted to know what was impeding its progress and it stared hard at Mr Darwin as if to say: what are you playing at? But it wasn't afraid. It hadn't yet learned to fear people.

James Island was the last one we visited. Mr Darwin was particularly interested in the finches. Their habits were varied. Some of them lived on cacti, and some on insects and leaves. Some stayed on the ground while others lived in the trees. Mr Darwin had them all sketched. He would lay out the drawings and point out the way they all had beaks suited to their particular diet. Some had long, pointy beaks while others had shorter, heavier ones. He sits watching the wildlife and smiles. As we sailed away from the islands, some of the officers told Mr Darwin that they had seen different birds and tortoises on different islands. This has given him food for thought. He calls the Galápagos the land that time forgot. I have a feeling it is a land he will remember all his life.

*Mr Darwin has preserved these reptiles in alcohol so they won't rot on the long journey home.*

# November 1835

We have almost completed the 3,200-mile voyage to Tahiti. The weather has been clear and bright and we have been racing along at the rate of 150 miles a day. The deck has been covered in tortoises brought on board during our stay in the Galápagos. Unfortunately, most of them are destined to become soup to feed the crew. We have passed rings of coral called lagoon islands. They have long, brilliant-white beaches. It is a wonder the way they rise so suddenly out of the vast ocean. Mr Darwin spent a long time looking at them, but he has vanished into his cabin. I am sure he already has his books spread out on the table and is trying to come up with an explanation for these astonishing formations.

At sunrise this morning we got our first glimpse of Tahiti. All of us have been looking forward to visiting these famous South Sea Islands, charted years ago by the great Captain Cook. From on deck I could see groves of coconut palms, breadfruit trees and banana plantations. The breakers crash onto jagged rocks, sending white sea spray high into the air. It is a scene straight out of a painting. As we sailed closer, I could see the Tahitians approaching in canoes, made from hollowed-out trees. Both the men and women are tattooed and wear garlands of coconut leaves around their heads. The women also have flowers in their hair. After breakfast, several of us rowed ashore.

Both Captain Fitzroy and Mr Darwin joined the party. We walked along a path through the palms. Huts were dotted among the trees and we could see the families going about their business. Some were using banana leaves as plates. Over the next few days Mr Fitzroy went about taking measurements of the coast. Some of us accompanied Mr Darwin on a trip into the interior of the island. We climbed steep slopes, having to edge along narrow paths. At one point magnificent waterfalls, two to three hundred feet high, cascaded around us. Nowhere on our journey have any of us seen more magnificent scenery. We ate roasted bananas and also sampled pineapples and coconut milk. Mr Darwin thought it was very refreshing, though I wasn't so sure about the taste. I prefer my milk from a cow.

*The ship's artist sketched these palm trees.*

On our return from exploring the centre of the island, we had an audience with Queen Pomare II. We will be sad to leave Tahiti. Everyone has been impressed by the way the people live in harmony with nature.

So here we are on the far side of the world. Soon, we will turn back towards England and make our way home. I think that Mr Darwin is growing homesick.

He is reading and re-reading the letters he has received from his sisters at our many ports of call. I think he is dreaming of the family home in Shrewsbury. Little wonder. It is four long years since we first left Plymouth. He is dreaming of England, the stories he is going to tell and the book he is going to write. The closer we come to the end of the *Beagle*'s voyage the more I think Mr Darwin must have changed his mind about entering the Church. With every day that passes, he is more drawn to the attractions of a scientific life. He has sent so many boxes back to England on our journey and written so many pages of notes. Can he really turn his back on them and settle into the life of a country vicar? I just don't believe it. He wants to be a geologist and naturalist.

It is even rumoured that Captain Fitzroy is preoccupied with thoughts of home. How I envy these gentlemen their family estates, mothers, fathers, brothers and sisters. How I would love to have a family of my own to return to. An orphan myself, the moment I return to England I will be looking to sign up for another few years at sea. While Mr Darwin will have his studies, I have nothing to keep me in England, no ties at all. The vast ocean is my home.

In the four years of our voyage so far, all
of us have changed. I am fourteen now,
and both stronger and wiser. Mr Darwin
was twenty-two when he first boarded
the *Beagle*. He is now in his twenty-sixth
year. He seems to have decided that his
hunting and shooting days are behind
him. It takes up time he could be spending
on other things. Surely that is another
sign that he is going to devote the rest
of his life to the study of nature.

Captain Fitzroy has given further
encouragement to Mr Darwin's future
career as nature's historian by suggesting
that he publishes his diary. Mr Darwin
seems very proud to have been asked.
He has also received good news from
home in his sisters' letters. The fossils
he sent back are being studied. Learned
men want to meet him. He is becoming
quite the celebrity, and I am sure he
has a great future ahead of him.

# WHAT HAPPENED NEXT?

From Tahiti, the *Beagle* sailed to New Zealand, then onward to Australia, where Darwin met some of the land's aboriginal people. He went on to explore coral reefs around the Keeling or Cocos Islands. From there, the *Beagle* continued as far as Mauritius and South Africa before turning home.

The ship arrived in Falmouth on 2 October 1836, almost five years since she had left England. On the way home, Darwin felt that the fields of England were greener than he remembered them. Feeling homesick, he left the ship as soon as the gangplank was down. He walked through the door of his Shrewsbury home, The Mount, three days later on Wednesday, 5 October.

The Beagle *approaching the port of St Louis in the Mauritius in April 1836.*

*The notes Darwin made on the Beagle voyage were the basis for his book,* Journal of Researches. *This book is now called* The Voyage of the Beagle.

Five years is a long time to be away from home. Darwin was changing, and he came home to a Britain that was also changing. Railways were spreading across the country. There were new factories springing up and the cities were growing. In June 1837, the Victorian era began as eighteen-year-old Queen Victoria, who would go on to reign for 64 years, came to the throne.

When Darwin left Plymouth in 1831, he was still thinking he might have a career in the Church. By the time he returned he believed in God, but he wasn't sure that the Old Testament told the whole truth about how the world was created. Influenced by what he had seen on his travels, he was slowly starting to gather his ideas. One day they would cause a great storm. People still argue about them today.

People were fascinated by Darwin the traveller and he attended many meetings with scientists. On 29 January 1839, he married his cousin, Emma, with whom he would have a large family. That same year his first book *Journal of Researches* was published as the third volume of Captain Robert Fitzroy's official account of the voyage. It was soon published on its own and made Darwin famous. The *Beagle*'s adventures caught the imagination of Victorian England. But Darwin wasn't content to describe the wonders of the natural world, he wanted to explain them.

This was in his famous theory of evolution.

*This portrait of Emma Darwin was made in 1840. Emma was the grand-daughter of Josiah Wedgwood, who was famous for his pottery.*

*Darwin's Zoology of the Voyage of HMS Beagle was published in five parts between 1838 and 1843. This illustration from the book shows Darwin's mouse, one of the many new species that Darwin found on his travels.*

When Darwin set off on his great journey across the world, most people believed that animals and plants were the way they had always been, created according to God's design. Darwin challenged this and said instead that living creatures were always changing and developing. Life was a struggle for survival. There was no great plan. The changes happened by chance. Those members of each living species which were best suited to their environment would pass their traits on to the next generation, leading to a gradual change of species. Darwin saw proof of this in his famous finches. From one original type of finch, a variety of different species would evolve through competition and come to live more successfully in their local environment.

*A vegetarian finch from the Galápagos Islands. This picture appeared in Darwin's* Zoology of the Voyage of HMS Beagle.

Darwin didn't rush to publish his ideas. His most famous book *On the Origin of Species* didn't come out until 24 November 1859, over twenty years after the *Beagle*'s return. The book caused a sensation and upset many Christians, who believed it challenged the idea of a human soul. Captain Fitzroy was one of the people who opposed Darwin.

*The Galápagos finches have different beaks, depending on the food they eat. Darwin saw this as proof that the birds had adapted to their habitat so they could survive. This illustration was published in Darwin's* Journal of Researches.

LARGE GROUND FINCH    MEDIUM GROUND FINCH    SMALL TREE FINCH    WARBLER FINCH

Darwin suffered repeated bouts of illness, but that didn't stop him producing more books that developed his theory of evolution. The idea that upset people most was that humans were the result of gradual changes from their ape ancestors. Darwin died on 19 April 1882 at the age of seventy-three. He had become one of the most famous men of his age. He was given a great funeral at Westminster Abbey, London, where he is buried.

In the years after Darwin's death, most scientists came to believe his views. Many people who believe in God argue that there can still be a Creator who designed nature. The argument will go on and on, but Charles Darwin changed the way we think about the world we live in.

*Darwin took a walk around his garden each day. This portrait was taken in the garden of his home, Down House, in 1881.*

*Charles and Emma Darwin, and their eight children, lived in Down House in the south-east of England from 1842 until Darwin's death in 1882. The house is now a museum and many artefacts from Darwin's Beagle voyage can be seen there.*

# HMS BEAGLE

This is the story of one of the most famous ships that ever sailed the seas. HMS *Beagle* was known as a brig, which is a sailing ship with two square-rigged masts. Brigs were fast and easy to manoeuvre and they were quite like the ships seen in pirate films. The *Beagle* weighed 242 tons and carried ten guns, though she only carried six during the famous second voyage when Darwin made his discoveries. She was 90 feet in length (about 30m). That is only slightly longer than a tennis court, so it must have been very cramped on board, with a crew of 74.

*The ship's crew of the HMS Beagle was painted by Augustus Earle around 1833. All 74 members of crew are here during a Bible reading in the gunroom.*

HMS *Beagle* was launched in 1820 from Woolwich dockyard on the river Thames, London. Nothing in the ship's early life hinted at the fame to come. She spent five years in reserve, waiting to be sent on a voyage. During this time, she was moored without masts or rigging. Eventually, in 1825, she was employed as a survey ship.

*This sketch of the inside of the Beagle in 1832 is based on a sketch by Midshipman King. He and Darwin slept in the chart room (top left).*

WHALE BOAT

CHART ROOM

MAIN MAST

CAPTAIN'S STOREROOM

CAPTAIN'S CABIN

GUNROOM

MIDSHIPMEN'S BERTH

BREAD ROOM

MIZZEN MAST

*HMS* Beagle *in 1841, painted during the third voyage while surveying Australia.*

In May 1826, she set sail to the southern coast of South America, during which Robert Fitzroy took charge of the HMS *Beagle*. He brought four Fuegians back to England, one of whom died after arriving in England in 1830. Fitzroy captained the second *Beagle* voyage (1831–1836), which brought the Fuegians home.

Before the *Beagle* set off on the famous second voyage, Captain Fitzroy arranged for her to be rebuilt – she was in very poor condition. The repairs almost amounted to more than it cost to build the ship originally, but Fitzroy wanted the ship to be in good shape for the voyage through the rough seas around the southern coast of South America. At his own cost he also used the most up-to-date instruments to help him on the voyage. This included twenty-two chronometers, which would help him navigate the seas, and five sympiesometers, which were like thermometers and barometers combined, and were to help Fitzroy judge the weather. Fitzroy later became a pioneer of accurate weather forecasting.

The third voyage of the *Beagle*, from 1837 to 1843, took her back to Australia, to survey the coast, and to Timor. Her captain named an area of north Australia Port Darwin, after the naturalist.

The ship was later used to control smuggling in the Thames estuary, UK. She was finally sold to scrap merchants and broken up in 1870.

CUTTER (BOAT)

FOREMAST

MEN'S MESS TABLES

SICK BAY

HOLD

COAL HOLE

WATER TANKS

# THE ROUTE OF DARWIN'S VOYAGE

**Darwin travelled on the second HMS *Beagle* voyage. Today we are used to travelling across the world by plane, so it is hard to imagine what an amazing journey it must have been. It lasted almost five years, from December 1831 to October 1836, and took in South America, the Falkland Islands, the Galápagos, Tahiti, New Zealand, Australia and South Africa.**

When anybody mentions the second voyage of the *Beagle* today, they usually think about Darwin's scientific discoveries, but it was originally meant to produce naval charts for war or trade. Captain Fitzroy surveyed the coasts of Patagonia (the southern coasts of Chile and Argentina) using smaller boats as well as the *Beagle* so that he could chart the small inlets and rivers that the *Beagle* was too large to survey.

It was a dangerous journey for the seas could be very rough, especially in the cold waters around Tierra del Fuego. There were many islands and rocks to manoeuvre around, and fearsome winds and large waves that could rise from out of nowhere. Whether for Fitzroy's thorough survey of the region or for Darwin's achievements, this voyage on the *Beagle* is an epic journey that will always be remembered.

ASIA

Cocos Islands

AUSTRALIA

Sydney

Albany

Hobart

New Zealand

# LIFE AT SEA

In the 19th century, life on a ship often meant years in cramped conditions away from home and family. The ship's crew became a sailor's family. Life at sea was dangerous, with stormy seas and slippery decks, not to mention disease from rats and other vermin that crept on board when the ship docked.

### Chain of command on the *Beagle*

Robert Fitzroy, the captain, was in charge of the ship. Below him were John Wickham (first lieutenant) and James Sullivan (second lieutenant). Beneath the second lieutenant came Midshipman Philip Gidley King. The name Midshipman comes from the parts of the ship where these officers were quartered. Senior commissioned officers had their quarters in the stern, midshipmen in the middle or midships, and the ordinary seamen in the forecastle, at the front. Other senior men included Robert McCormick (the surgeon), Benjamin Benoe (the assistant surgeon) and George Rowlett (the purser, who was in charge of handling money on board).

### What were the jobs on the ship?

The surgeon was in charge of the men's health and the parson looked after the religious welfare of the crew. There was also a cook, a boatswain (in charge of the sails), a carpenter and a quartermaster, who was in charge of navigating the ship. The remaining crew members had to keep watch, handle the sails and clean the decks.

*One of Darwin's surveying instruments on the* Beagle.

### Free time

There was a strong sense of comradeship. The men liked to drink ale together, and enjoyed playing dice and cards. They told tales, sang sea-shanties and played music. Some liked carving, practising tying knots, drawing and making ship models. When the senior crew members allowed it, the sailors played practical jokes on the officers. This was only on special occasions though, such as Crossing the Line (see page 16). At other times, they could be punished for bad behaviour.

*Crew members were highly skilled at unfurling sails on the masts and climbing rigging. It was hard and dangerous work.*

## Punishment

The captain and his senior officers maintained strict discipline on the ship. Crew members were flogged for misbehaving, or put into leg-irons. The punishments were often carried out in front of all on the ship to remind crew members to behave.

## Sleeping

The crew slept below decks in hammocks or cradles suspended from the ceiling. They were very close together, and the hammocks rocked with the motion of the ship, which caused Darwin to suffer from seasickness. The hammocks could be rolled up during the day to create more space on the ship.

## Health

There was a lot of sickness at sea. The seamen were often cold and wet, and the rats carried diseases. A lack of vitamin C could lead to a disease called scurvy, so the crew had to collect fruit, which is rich in vitamin C, whenever the ship docked. The ship's surgeon took care of any ill crew members in the sick bay.

## Food on board

The food on a ship was often poor quality. Salt and pork was salted to preserve them so the food would keep well on the long voyage. The seafarers' diet also included cheese, fish, ale and hard, dried biscuits. The crew ate local fresh fruit and meat whenever the ship docked. During the voyage of the *Beagle*, the men ate the animals they had captured, even the poor tortoises! The tortoises were gathered up in their hundreds and provided fresh food for the crew while at sea.

*The giant tortoises of the Galápagos Islands provided a great meal for the sailors. They were caught and kept on board to eat during long sea voyages.*

# DARWIN'S SPECIMENS

All scientists have to collect evidence to support their theories. Darwin was away from England for almost five years. In that time he collected an enormous number of specimens of animals, plants, rocks and fossils.

## Collecting methods

In his writings, Darwin describes how he collected his specimens. He lifted up stones and rocks to find the creatures beneath, and kept them in jars. Other animals were captured in forests, and many were killed. Sometimes, the animals would be dissected. Darwin also fished for plankton, jellyfish and other creatures with iron and gauze nets. He would dry plants and keep them in special drying paper. Small creatures were kept in bottles, which Darwin filled with spirit and chemicals to preserve them. The larger animals and fossils were placed into barrels or wooden boxes, which the crew had to make.

These pill boxes belonging to Darwin were used to contain small specimens.

## Identifying specimens

Darwin kept a log book of his specimens, as well as tagging and numbering them all and making notes about the location and time of discovery or capture. Fossil bones were cleaned and numbered so that they could be assembled properly back home. To help identify his finds, Darwin consulted books written by the experts of the day, and he also wrote to them directly about his discoveries.

A note written by Charles Darwin about evolution. It was through his notes and examining his specimens that Darwin formed his theories.

*Fossilized bones, such as these Macrauchenia foot bones, formed a large and important part of Darwin's specimen collection.*

## A man of letters

Whenever the *Beagle* moored at a town, Darwin's letters were sent to England. Ships brought back letters from the finest geologists, zoologists, botanists and naturalists. It took a long time, but it was a very important way of confirming that he had found a new species.

## Sending specimens home

Whenever the *Beagle* interrupted its voyage to allow Darwin to explore, or to make repairs to the ship, the crew would load many boxes and barrels onto ships bound for England. This included the dried flower collections, the many jars of preserved creatures and huge boxes full of fossilized bones, teeth and skulls. From these remains the scientists back in England would recognize extinct creatures such as the Megatherium and the Hoplophorus.

## What happened to the specimens?

On Darwin's return to England he allowed various scientists to take his specimens to study. Some stayed in their cabinets for many years. Eventually they were sold and donated to the great museums, such as the Natural History Museum in London, England.

*Specimens collected by Charles Darwin are now held by the Natural History Museum in London.*

# 19TH~CENTURY SCIENTISTS

Darwin was one of many important 19th-century scientists. This was an era of great scientific invention and discovery. There were significant achievements in mathematics, biology, chemistry, astronomy, physics and medicine.

## Questioning the world

The naturalists of the 19th century gathered information to investigate how the world worked. There were many theories and often there were disagreements within the scientific community, but their discoveries ultimately paved the way for a greater understanding of our planet.

*Sir Charles Lyell* (1797–1875) was a Scottish geologist who argued that the changes that happen to the Earth around us occur slowly and gradually over millions of years, not in a series of sudden catastrophes. He is painted here in Down House standing between Sir Joseph Hooker (1817–1911), an English botanist and explorer, and Charles Darwin (left).

Swiss born *Louis Agassiz* (1807–1873) was a zoologist and geologist who investigated glaciers and the history of the ice age. He later settled in the USA.

The German biologist and physician *Ernst Haeckel* (1834–1919) named thousands of new species. There are mountains in the USA and New Zealand named after him.

*Roderick Murchison*
*(1792–1871) was a Scottish*
*geologist. He investigated*
*the Silurian and Devonian*
*systems, which are*
*geological time periods*
*in Earth's history.*

*Sir Richard Owen (1804–1892),*
*an English scientist, was the*
*most important anatomist of his*
*day. He put forward the idea*
*that the way an animal lived*
*could be deduced by its shape*
*and internal organs. He coined*
*the term 'dinosauria', which later*
*became dinosaur. He's pictured*
*here with a skeleton of a giant*
*moa, an extinct bird.*

There were many other eminent biologists
and geologists in the 19th century.

**Georges Cuvier** (1769–1832) was a French
scientist, known as the father of vertebrate
palaeontology. He classified living and fossil
creatures according to their similarities.

**Jean-Baptiste Lamarck** (1744–1829), a French
scientist, was an early believer in the idea that
evolution developed according to natural laws.
He was a pioneer of botany and biology.

**Othniel Charles Marsh** (1831–1899) was an
American professor of palaeontology at Yale
University, USA. He discovered about eighty
new types of dinosaur, demonstrating the
huge variety of fossil life.

# MORE 19TH-CENTURY SCIENTISTS

**A changing era**

The era in which Darwin lived was a time of great change. As the naturalists and geologists strived to understand the creatures and history of the planet, other scientists were making progress in medicine, electricity, technology and astronomy. New inventions in the form of machines and processes started to make changes in people's lives, from pasteurized milk to electric lighting.

*Michael Faraday (1791–1867) was an English chemist and physicist. He studied electricity and magnetism. He discovered benzene and invented an early form of the Bunsen burner.*

*The French chemist Louis Pasteur (1822–1895) made important discoveries in microbiology. He created the first vaccine for rabies and developed the process of pasteurization to stop milk going sour.*

*Hermann von Helmholtz (1821–1894) was a German physicist and physician. He made important discoveries in physiology and electro-magnetism.*

There were many other eminent 19th-century physicists, mathematicians and astronomers.

**Joseph Henry** (1797–1878) was an American scientist who became the first secretary of the Smithsonian Institution. He worked in the field of electro-magnetism.

German-born **Caroline Herschel** (1750–1848) worked with her brother Sir William as an astronomer. She discovered several comets and catalogued many stars.

**Sonia Kovalevsky** (1850–1891) was the first major female Russian mathematician.

*William Thomson, Lord Kelvin* (1824–1907) was an Irish-born physicist and engineer who did important work in physics. He developed the Kelvin scale of temperature measurement.

*This was a time when few women became scientists. The lady pictured here, **Maria Mitchell** (1818–1889), was the first professional woman astronomer in the United States. In the UK, Mary Somerville (1780–1872) and Caroline Herschel were leading figures in astronomy, and were the first women to become members of the Royal Astronomical Society.*

# EXTINCT CREATURES

The idea of extinction (species dying out altogether) was accepted only in the late 18th century. It is caused by many things, such as hunting or loss of habitat. Darwin's theory of evolution explained that extinction is a part of natural selection – where, over time, some animals adapt and survive, others decline in numbers and some become extinct. Some extinct animals are shown here. A mass extinction around 65 million years ago, most likely because of a meteor impact, wiped out around fifty per cent of the world's species (including the dinosaurs) in a short time.

**Trilobite**
*When*: 542–250 million years ago
*Where*: worldwide
*Size*: average 2–7cm long
*Diet*: Some of these creatures were scavengers. Some swam and fed on plankton.

**Hyracotherium** (Hyrax beast)
*When*: about 50 million years ago
*Where*: Asia, Europe, North America
*Size*: average 60cm long
*Diet*: leaves
This was the earliest member of the horse family. It was the size of a hare and had teeth designed for eating leaves from bushes.

**Phorusrhacos** (Terror bird)
*When*: 27 million–15,000 years ago
*Where*: South America
*Size*: 2.5m tall
*Diet*: large animals
A fast runner, this bird could outrun most of its prey. It was a kind of giant, flesh-eating ostrich.

**Macrauchenia** (Big llama)
*When*: 7 million–10,000 years ago
*Where*: South America
*Size*: 2m tall
*Diet*: ground plants
This animal was long-legged,
long-necked and had a trunk.

**Smilodon**
(Sabre-tooth tiger)
*When*: 2.5 million–
10,000 years ago
*Where*: North America
and South America
*Size*: 2m long
*Diet*: big mammals
This animal evolved to kill
the big plant-eaters of the time.

**Glyptodon**
*When*: 2.5 million–
10,000 years ago
*Where*: North America
and South America
*Size*: about 3m long
*Diet*: low plants
This was a large
armadillo-like animal
from South America.

**Megatherium**
*When*: 2 million–
8,000 years ago
*Where*: North,
Central and South
America
*Size*: 3m tall
*Diet*: trees
This was a giant
sloth that evolved
in South America.

# GLOSSARY

**anatomist**
A person who studies the body structures of plants or animals.

**astronomer**
A scientist who studies the stars and the universe.

**barometer**
An instrument used to measure air pressure.

**benefactor**
A person who helps another, especially by giving money.

**berth**
A cabin on a ship.

**botanist**
A scientist who studies plants.

**bow**
A name for the front of a ship.

**brig**
A type of ship that is fast and easy to manoeuvre.

**cat-o'-nine-tails**
A whip with nine knotted rope or leather ends.

**caulk**
To seal and make watertight the wooden planks of a ship.

**chart**
To note coastlines, currents and sea depths to create a sea map (also called a chart).

**Crossing the Line**
A ceremony on a ship to celebrate a person's first crossing of the Equator. The event is overseen by a person dressed as Neptune, the king of the sea. Traditionally, the officers of the ship let the sailors take over for the duration of the ceremony.

**dissect**
To take apart in order to see the internal workings of something.

**embedded**
Stuck firmly inside something.

**Equator**
An imaginary line around the centre of the Earth, which runs through the tropical (hot and usually wet) regions.

**evolution**
The process of change from one generation to the next.

**extinct**
When all animals of a species die, and none are left.

**finch**
A type of small bird. Darwin studied the many different finch species in the Galápagos.

**flogging**
Whipping with the end of a rope or a cat-o'-nine-tails.

**forecastle**
The part of the ship, above and below decks, that is in front of the foremast.

**fossil**
The remains of ancient animals or plants that have turned to rock.

**gaucho**
A horseman of the South American pampas.

**gauze**
A thin, see-through fabric. When used in a net, it allows water to drain, leaving creatures behind.

**geologist**
A scientist who studies the surface, life and history of the Earth.

**hereditary**
Passed down from one generation to the next, such as from parents to their children.

**Hoplophorus**
A kind of Glyptodon, which was a large armadillo-like animal.

**instrument maker**
The instrument maker on the HMS *Beagle* was employed by the captain to look after the ship's navigational equipment.

**Mastodon**
An elephant-like animal that lived in Europe, Asia and North America thousands of years ago.

**Megatherium**
A type of elephant-sized ground sloth that lived in America from 2 million to 8,000 years ago.

**missionary**
A person sent on a mission, especially to do religious or charitable work.

**naturalist**
A scientist who studies living things.

**palaeontology**
The study of prehistoric life through the examination of fossils.

**pampas**
The vast, flat grasslands of lowland South America.

**parasite**
A plant or animal living on or feeding off another living thing and doing it harm.

**physicist**
A scientist who studies the forces of the Earth, such as electricity and heat.

**pioneer**
Someone who opens up a new area of thought or research, or who goes into unknown areas.

**plankton**
Tiny sea animals or plants that float in the ocean and are the main food for many sea animals.

**preserve**
To keep from rotting.

**rigging**
The network of ropes that helps to hold up a ship's masts and allows her sails to be controlled.

**sanctuary**
A safe place.

**scurvy**
A disease of the skin and gums caused by a lack of vitamin C.

**sea-shanty**
A rhythmic song that helped sailors pass their day-to-day activities on a ship.

**shackled**
Chained up using a type of heavy chain called a shackle.

**stern**
The rear of a ship.

**surveying**
Measuring an area of land, such as a coastline, to make a map of it.

**tamarind**
A sour, tropical fruit that grows in Africa and Asia.

**theory**
A scientist's explanation of something.

**thumbscrew**
An instrument of torture used by some slave-owners in the 19th century. It slowly crushed a person's thumbs.

**trawl**
A wide-mouthed net, which is dragged through water to catch creatures.

**vermin**
Small animals and insects that do harm, for example by carrying diseases.

**vertebrate**
An animal that has an internal skeleton.

## MEASUREMENTS

The lengths, weights and distances in the diary are in old, or imperial, measurements, which James would have used. Use this guide to convert the old measurements into modern, or metric, lengths, distances and weights:

**feet**
A measure of length. Multiply by 0.3048 to find out a length in metres.

**miles**
A measure of distance. Multiply the number of miles by 1.61 to find out a distance in kilometres.

**pounds**
A measure of weight. Multiply by 0.454 to find out a weight in kilograms.

**tons**
A measure of weight. Multiply by 0.907 to find out the weight in metric tonnes.

# INDEX

# ACKNOWLEDGEMENTS

The publisher would like to thank the following for permission to reproduce their material. Every care has been taken to trace copyright holders. However, if there have been unintentional omissions or failure to trace copyright holders, we apologize and will, if informed, endeavour to make corrections in any future edition.

Key: *b* = bottom, *c* = centre, *l* = left, *r* = right, *t* = top

Pages 2*tr* English Heritage/Down House, Kent; 2*cr* Science Photo Library (SPL)/Barbara Strnadova; 2*br* Natural History Museum, London; 4*tl* English Heritage/Down House, Kent; 4*l* iStockphoto; 4*bc* Natural History Museum, London; 4*br* Natural History Museum, London; 8 iStockphoto; 8*tr* Natural History Museum, London; 13*r* Getty/Dorling Kindersley; 14*t* Natural History Museum, London; 14*cl* Oxford University of Natural History/Darwin database; 15*tr* National Maritime Museum, London; 15*cr* National Maritime Museum, London; 16*l* iStockphoto; 17*tr* Frank lane Picture Agency/Ronald Thompson; 18*tr* Natural History Museum, London; 22*tl* Lyndon Baines Johnson Library and Museum, Austin, Texas; 22*cl* Photolibrary/Christopher Fairweather; 24 Natural History Museum, London; 26*cl* Corbis/David Stoecklein; 27*t* Bridgeman Art Library/Giraudon; 27*r* Photolibrary/Steve Cole; 32*cl* Alamy/Andrew Linscott; 33*cr* Heritage Image Partnership (HIP)/Ann Ronan Picture Library; 33*br* UBC Botanical Garden and Centre for Plant Research, Vancouver, Canada; 34*cl* iStockphoto; 34*br* Natural History Museum, London; 36 Alamy/David Frazier; 38*lc* University of Cambridge; 42 Alamy/Mary Evans Picture Library; 43*t* Bridgeman Art Library/Down House; 43*b* Natural History Museum, London; 44*tl* Alamy/Natural History Museum, London; 44*b* Bridgeman Art Library/Down House; 45*tl* Natural History Museum, London; 45*tr* Bridgeman Art Library; 45*r* HIP/Ann Ronan Picture Library; 45*b* Corbis/David Ball; 46*tr* National Maritime Museum, London; 48 English Heritage/Down House; 48–49 iStockphoto; 50 English Heritage/Down House; 51 Alamy/fotoNatura; 52*tr* English Heritage/Down House; 52*c* Natural History Museum, London; 52*br* Getty/Hulton; 53*tl*, 52*c* Natural History Museum, London; 53*br*, 52*c* Natural History Museum, London; 54*tr* Bridgeman Art Library; 54*c* SPL/Marine Biological Laboratory; 54*bl* Getty/Hulton; 55*tl* Corbis/Hulton; 55*b* SPL/George Bernard; 56*l* Getty/Time Life; 56*tr* Getty/Hulton; 56*br* Heidelberg University, Germany; 57*tr* SPL/Royal Astronomical Society; 57*br* Science & Society Picture Library; 58*tr* Natural History Museum, London; 58*cl* Natural History Museum, London; 59*tl* Natural History Museum, London; 59*c* Natural History Museum, London; 59*br* Natural History Museum, London; 64 Ardea